AIRCRAFT

D1321964

A Piccolo Factbook

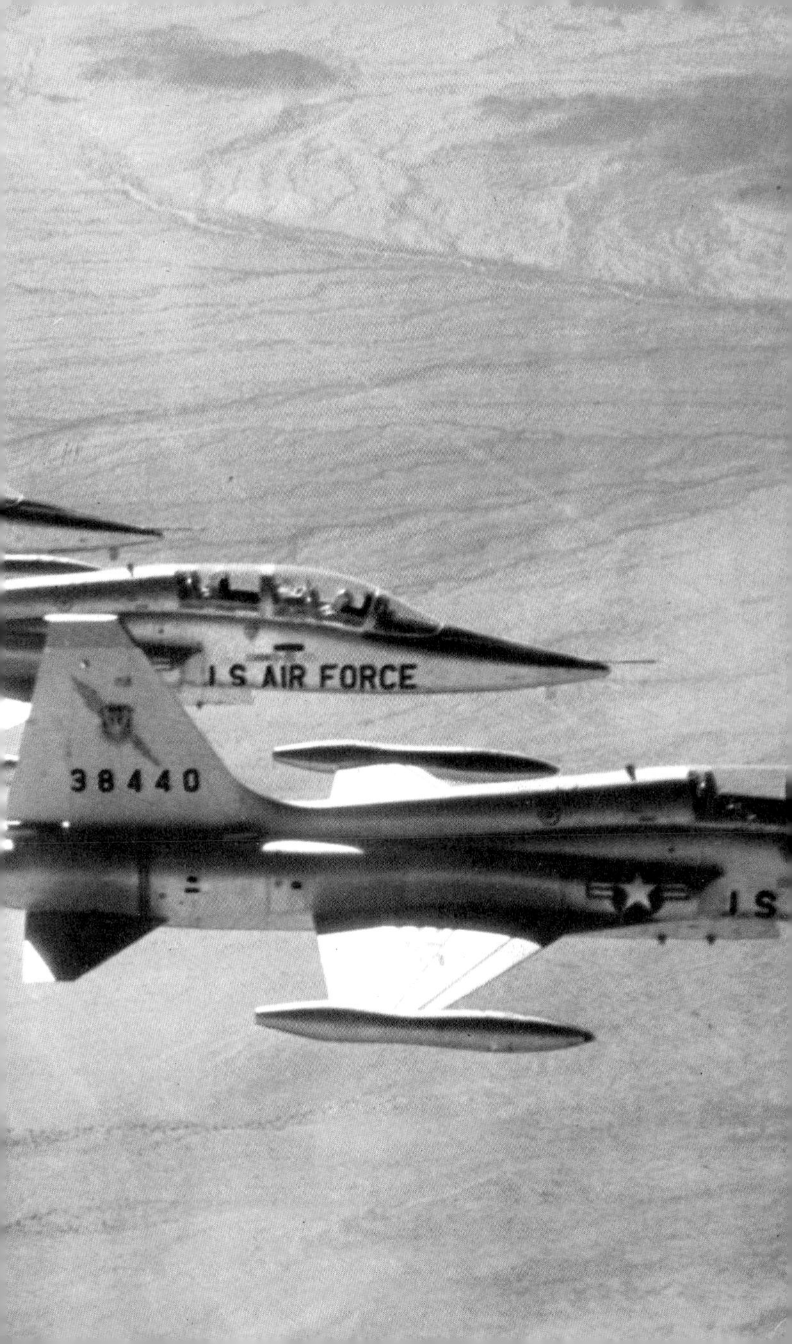

I.S AIR FORCE
38440
I.S

Contents

AIRCRAFT

By Chris Maynard
and John Paton

Series Design: David Jefferis

A Piccolo Factbook

The Flying Machines

For thousands of years, people have envied the ability of birds to soar through the air. Taking a lesson from nature, they even tried to copy birds by strapping crude wings to their arms and leaping off hills and high buildings. But none of these efforts ever amounted to much. No matter how hard human beings flapped, they could never stay airborne. They did not realize that human muscles are simply too weak, and their bodies too heavy, to stay aloft.

Learning About Flight

Early 'birdmen' simply did not understand the basic principles of flight. They did not know that the reason why birds can fly is that their wings are designed as 'aerofoils' to generate *lift* as they move forward through the air. Nor did they comprehend that the sculling action of the wingtip feathers provides the *thrust* which drives birds through the air.

Understanding wing shapes led to the first successes with flying machines. In 1894 the *Eole* (below), a man-carrying steam-powered machine, carried its pilot for a 49-metre hop just 20 cm above the ground.

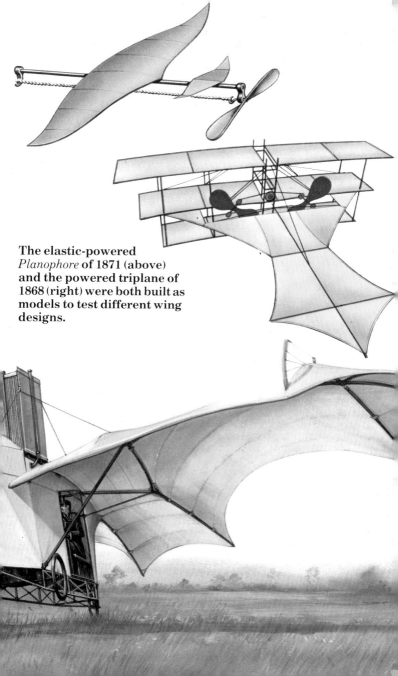

The elastic-powered
Planophore of 1871 (above)
and the powered triplane of
1868 (right) were both built as
models to test different wing
designs.

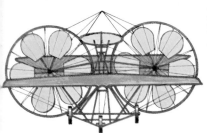

The first person to recognize how the wing of a bird worked was Sir George Cayley. He understood that to make any kind of aeroplane, it was first necessary to design a craft that was capable of gliding.

His breakthrough came in 1804 when he found that the surface of a kite provides lift. He built the world's first glider by attaching a kite to a long stick, adding a movable tail to steer it and a small weight in front for balance. It was launched from a steep hill and sailed down with great success. Later, Cayley sent his terrified coachman aloft in a full-sized glider. The coachman is said to have resigned on landing.

Cayley understood that the next stage was to find a source of power that would provide the thrust to propel his craft steadily forward. Unfortunately, there was no engine small enough and light enough in his time to solve this problem. William Henson, who had studied Cayley's gliders, produced a design for the world's first powered aeroplane in 1843; but he still lacked the engine to make a working model.

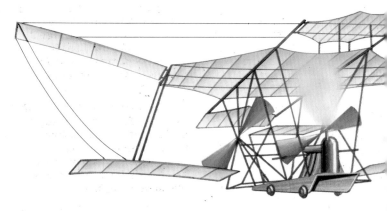

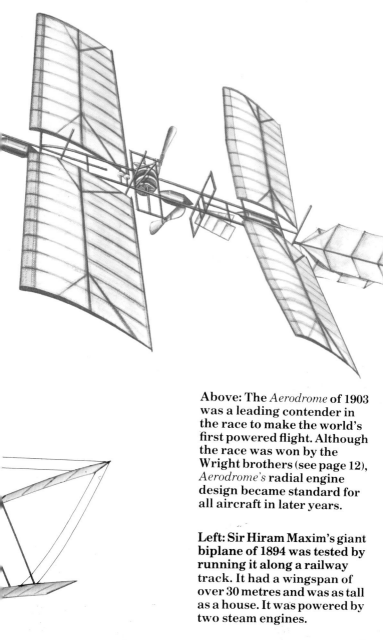

Above: The *Aerodrome* of 1903 was a leading contender in the race to make the world's first powered flight. Although the race was won by the Wright brothers (see page 12), *Aerodrome's* radial engine design became standard for all aircraft in later years.

Left: Sir Hiram Maxim's giant biplane of 1894 was tested by running it along a railway track. It had a wingspan of over 30 metres and was as tall as a house. It was powered by two steam engines.

Test Glides

The failure of the first powered aircraft to achieve anything more than shaky hops led some aviators to realize that a lot of testing was still needed. They turned to gliders, which were easy to build, to study the problems of design and control.

The most famous of the glider pilots was Otto Lilienthal of Germany. In the 1890s he made hundreds of flights, each time learning a little more about the way an aircraft could be balanced and controlled in the air. As Lilienthal wrote, 'to design a flying-machine is nothing; to build it is not much; to test it is everything.'

One of Lilienthal's designs (below) shows him hang-gliding with a massive biplane contraption. He controlled it by swinging his body to and fro. Unfortunately, he died in a crash before he could fit engines to his machines. However, Lilienthal's experimental flights inspired the Wright brothers in America.

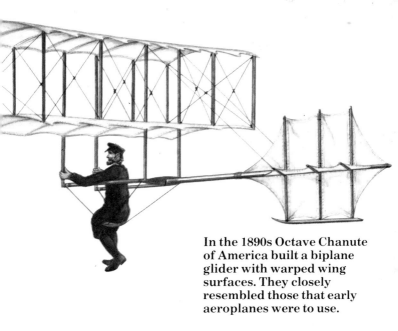

In the 1890s Octave Chanute of America built a biplane glider with warped wing surfaces. They closely resembled those that early aeroplanes were to use.

The Wright Brothers

Early aviators had to learn their trade from scratch. There was nobody who could teach them anything about the shape of an aeroplane wing or how to keep a flying-machine from crashing. They had to start with the basics.

Wilbur and Orville Wright approached the problem by first building a kite which they flew at Kitty Hawk, a site on the North Carolina sea coast where the wind was strong and steady. Having studied the way the kite handled, they proceeded to build a series of gliders. By the time they had reached their third model, in 1902, they had a shape that seemed to work. The main wings were warped to improve the flow of air over them, the rudder was at the back and the elevator surfaces at the front. With this design, they were able to control the glider and make a smooth, banked turn without plummeting to the ground.

Dozens of test flights helped them to iron out the kinks in its controls.

Now came the acid test – to make a controlled and powered flight that would carry a man. The Wright brothers worked long and hard at this.

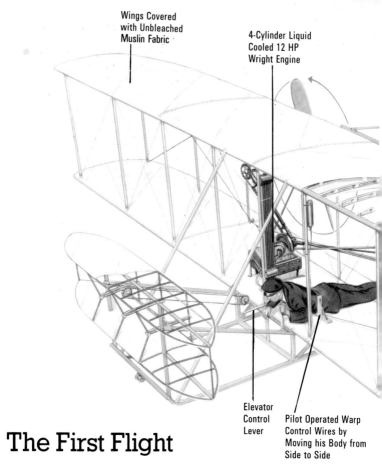

Wings Covered with Unbleached Muslin Fabric

4-Cylinder Liquid Cooled 12 HP Wright Engine

Elevator Control Lever

Pilot Operated Warp Control Wires by Moving his Body from Side to Side

The First Flight

On December 14, 1903, the Wright brothers' *Flyer* took off on a test flight. It climbed too steeply, stalled and crashed.

Three days later, the repairs having being made, Orville climbed on board and tried again. With his brother Wilbur running alongside to steady the wing, the plane accelerated to 13 km/h. Moving into a strong wind it took off, flew 37 metres, and bumped down again. Three more flights were made that day, the longest lasting under a minute and covering 260 metres. The age of powered flight had begun!

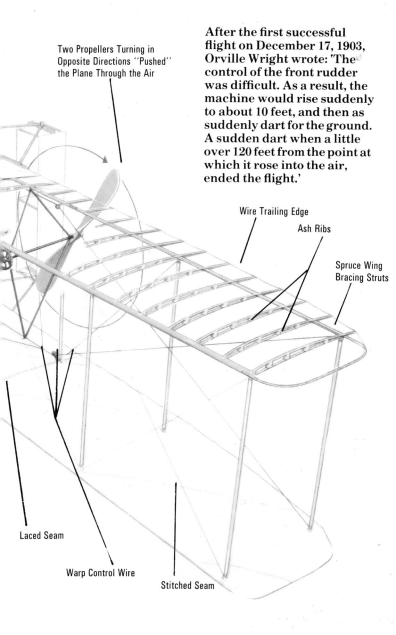

Two Propellers Turning in Opposite Directions "Pushed" the Plane Through the Air

After the first successful flight on December 17, 1903, Orville Wright wrote: 'The control of the front rudder was difficult. As a result, the machine would rise suddenly to about 10 feet, and then as suddenly dart for the ground. A sudden dart when a little over 120 feet from the point at which it rose into the air, ended the flight.'

Wire Trailing Edge

Ash Ribs

Spruce Wing Bracing Struts

Laced Seam

Warp Control Wire

Stitched Seam

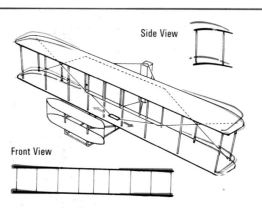

Side View

Front View

By warping, or twisting, its wing-tips, the *Flyer* could be controlled in the air. When one end of the wing was raised, the other end was lowered. The aircraft turned in the direction of the lower wing-tip. The pilot controlled the warping by pulling wires. To later aircraft, ailerons replaced wing-warping.

Convincing the World

The Wright brothers' historic flights in 1903 were hardly noticed by the world. The Wrights were secretive; they feared that others would copy their design. When they finally did invite the press to watch their *Flyer II* in 1904, a fault with the engine only increased the general disbelief. Even as late as 1906, *The Times* of Britain was still claiming that powered flight was impossible from an engineering standpoint.

However, the Wrights soon came back with a successful model, the *Flyer III*, which astounded the world with its manoeuvrability. With it they were able to make regular flights of over 32 km and in 1908 set a record of 124 km in a non-stop trip lasting almost 2½ hours. In Europe they astonished people with the plane's controls, for experimenters there had not even realized that special controls were needed to make a plane work! In September 1908, Orville crashed his biplane, and killed a US Army lieutenant. This first flying fatality dampened the brothers' enthusiasm.

Right: Wilbur Wright (above) and Orville Wright (below) ran a bicycle-making business in Dayton, Ohio. Their boyhood interest in flying led them to test kites and then gliders to find the right wing shape for an aeroplane. They also designed and built a lightweight 12 hp petrol engine to power it. Strangely enough, after five years of success, both brothers lost interest in flying.

Below: This photograph, taken on December 17, 1903, shows Orville Wright at the controls of the world's first successful aircraft. During the first flight, the machine was airborne for 12 seconds and reached a maximum altitude of 3 metres.

Early Flight in Europe

For a time after 1906, France seemed to become the home of aviation. After the early American successes, the focus of world attention shifted there.

The Brazilian pioneer aviator, Alberto Santos-Dumont, became the first person in Europe to make a powered flight in November 1906, with his bizarre-looking craft the *14 bis*. The plane flew tail-first, and looked for all the world as if it were travelling backward.

Control of a plane by wing-warping had been replaced with control by the use of ailerons, which allow parts of the wings to move up and down. The *14 bis* had octagonal ailerons in the outer wing 'boxes', linked to a harness worn by the pilot. To control them, Santos-Dumont simply leaned to the left or to the right.

Another strange craft was the bamboo and canvas *Demoiselle* of 1907, also built by Santos-Dumont. It was a light, cheap 'do-it-yourself' affair, but once assembled, it could fly at almost 97 km/h.

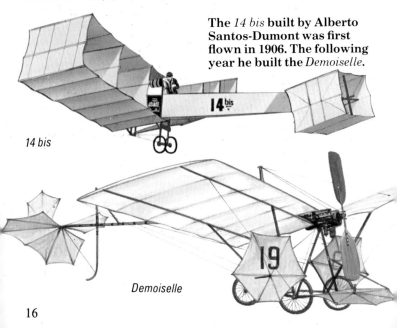

The *14 bis* built by Alberto Santos-Dumont was first flown in 1906. The following year he built the *Demoiselle*.

14 bis

Demoiselle

Above: Glenn Curtiss' *Golden Flyer* **won the speed trophy at the world's first air race at Rheims in 1909.**

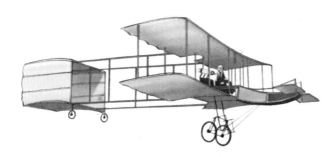

Above: The *Bird of Passage* **(1909) – a successful flying machine – built by Gabriel and Charles Voisin – the first commercial aircraft builders.**

Below: The aviator Henry Farman, designed a biplane known as Type III, which won the London to Manchester prize in 1910.

Crossing the Channel

With great fanfare, Louis Blériot set off from Calais (below) on July 25, 1909 to cross the English Channel. His home-made aircraft was a single-winged affair, driven by an air-cooled engine that could develop a speed of about 65 km/h.

Soon after take-off the weather became bad and, without a compass, Blériot became completely lost. For ten long minutes he flew alone with not even a ship to guide his way. Nor was his altitude sufficient to keep him constantly in sight of land. At last he caught sight of the English coast and continued on to make a safe but bumpy landing in a field near Dover Castle (right). His flight electrified the world and won him a £1000 prize from the *Daily Mail* newspaper. He had made the crossing in just 38 minutes.

Balloons and Airships

The Montgolfiers' hot-air balloon used a fire to give it lift. The passengers had to keep dowsing the fabric with water to keep it from bursting into flames.

In 1785, Blanchard and Jefferies crossed the English Channel in a hydrogen-filled balloon. They 'rowed' it across with air paddles, and steered with a giant rudder.

The first balloons that were big enough to carry passengers appeared in 1783. In that year the Montgolfier brothers, Etienne and Joseph, built a balloon that was filled with hot air from a fire in the basket slung beneath the envelope.

The first test pilots to make this great step for mankind were a sheep, a duck and a cock. Later that year human passengers rode in the Montgolfier balloon. Also in that year another French aviation pioneer, Jacques Charles, flew in the first hydrogen-filled balloon.

The big trouble with balloons is that they drift at the

mercy of the wind. Their ungainly shape also makes them very difficult to manoeuvre. The solution to the problem was to streamline their shape and to give them controls and a source of power.

The First Airship
The first person to try this was Henri Giffard. In 1852 he took a cigar-shaped balloon, filled it with hydrogen and fastened a small steam engine to it. His craft was the **first true airship, but it could not steer against the wind.**

At the end of the 19th century, the first designs for a rigid airship began to appear. It had an internal skeleton around which an envelope of fabric or metal sheeting could be fastened. Inside were giant gas bags that gave the craft its lift.

The Zeppelins
The famous airship designer and builder, Graf von Zeppelin, built a series of giant airships in the years before and after World War I. They introduced the world's first passenger air service and, later, the first transatlantic service.

The best airships were the giant *Graf Zeppelin* and the luxurious *Hindenburg* of the 1930s. The former was 235 metres long and could carry 20 passengers and a crew of 40 from Europe to New York in first-class luxury.

Military Airships
During World War I, the Zeppelin airships were converted to military use – they became the first strategic bombers (below). Raids were made on London by these big ships.

World War I

At the outbreak of World War I in 1914, few people had ever seen a plane, let alone thought of them as fighting machines. None carried any weapons at first. Their main use was as

scouts since they could cross enemy lines with ease. Aircrews took photographs of battlefield positions and used signals to direct the aim of artillery fire onto the enemy.

Perhaps inevitably, flyers took to dropping grenades and small hand-held bombs and to firing pistols at each other. Very soon, the sky too, became a battlefield.

A World War I aerial 'dogfight'. A German Albatros (far left) swoops down on a British SE5.

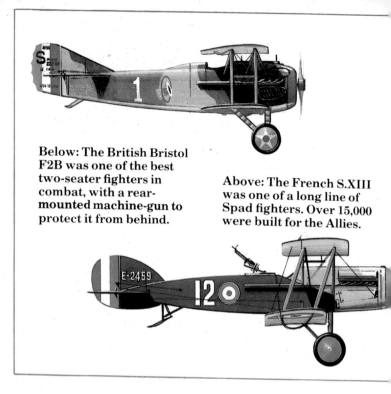

Below: The British Bristol F2B was one of the best two-seater fighters in combat, with a rear-mounted machine-gun to protect it from behind.

Above: The French S.XIII was one of a long line of Spad fighters. Over 15,000 were built for the Allies.

The First Fighters

Within a year of the outbreak of the war, aircraft were being fitted with machine-guns. But firing a gun from a moving plane was no easy task. The only way to shoot accurately was to mount the gun facing straight ahead. You then simply pointed the whole plane and fired.

The problem with this was that the bullets tended to hit the plane's propeller. It was a Dutch designer called Anthony Fokker, who was working for Germany, who came up with a solution. He linked the propeller to the gun's trigger so that the gun only fired when the blade was not in the way. The first true fighter-planes were born.

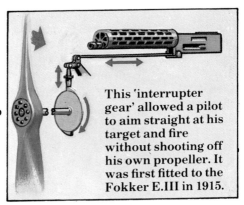

Below: The Fokker D.VII, flown by the Germans, was one of the best fighters of the war. It had a top speed of 185 km/h and could climb to 4900 metres in 16 minutes.

This 'interrupter gear' allowed a pilot to aim straight at his target and fire without shooting off his own propeller. It was first fitted to the Fokker E.III in 1915.

Flying 'Aces'

Fighter pilots fought as lone hunters or in massed formations. When two formations met they broke up into individual battles, known as 'dog-fights'. Pilots whirled and manoeuvred to get into close range and fire a burst of bullets at each other. They needed to perform complicated loops and rolls to enable them to change direction quickly.

Since few pilots ever wore parachutes, and since a single bullet or even a breakdown of their far-from-reliable engines could send them plunging to earth, the fighting life of a pilot was very brief, usually a matter of weeks. A great deal of courage was required to fight in this way, and pilots who managed to stay alive and shoot down a number of enemy planes became national heroes.

The Bombers Arrive

The notion of a large plane crammed with bombs, which could fly halfway across Europe and drop its cargo on an undefended city, filled people with horror when the first bombers were invented in World War I.

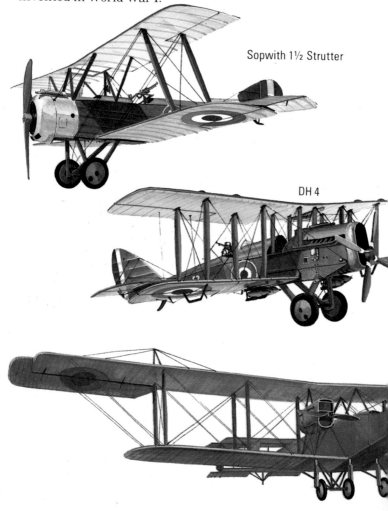

Sopwith 1½ Strutter

DH 4

Bombers gave war in the air a new dimension. In the past no nation could attack far in the rear of an enemy without first pushing back its armies. Now, for the first time, there was a weapon that could rain down bombs on railways, factories and towns. Defenceless citizens were thrust into the front line of attack.

A New Threat

In World War I, it was the threat of the bombers rather than the actual devastation they caused that outraged people. For example, in the first raid on a major city only five bombs were dropped. The raid took place over Paris in 1914. One person was killed and two were injured. The accuracy with which the heavy bombers could aim remained very poor, in spite of the fact that they were able to carry a two-tonne load by the end of the war.

Voisin

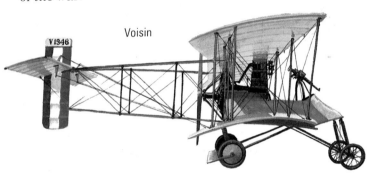

Handley Page 0/100

Two of Britain's best light bombers of World War I were the Sopwith 1½ Strutter and the DH4. However, their slow speed made them easy prey for fighters. One of the first light bombers of the war was the French Voisin. The HP 0/100 was a British heavy bomber which could carry almost two tonnes of bombs.

Left: The two-engined German Gotha G.IV had a top speed of 144 km/h and carried a load of almost 500 kg.

Above left: The Zeppelin-Staaken R.VI. This huge four-engined bomber had a wingspan of more than 42 metres.

Left: The three-engined Caproni Ca5 was an Italian medium bomber. It was used in 1918 to strike at military targets across the Alps in Austria, but it did not have the range to hit Vienna.

Big Bombers

In the 52 German bomber raids on London in World War I, 196 tonnes of bombs were dropped, killing 857 people and injuring over 2000 others. Although this was but a drop in the ocean compared to the havoc on the battlefields of France, it stirred up public anger to an intense degree – exactly the opposite of the terror intended.

A Rain of Death

The most widely used bomber was the Gotha G.IV. From June 1917 to May 1918 it flew in day and night raids on London. Because it could fly at the great height of 6450 metres it could escape fighter interception.

The first raid by Gothas was totally unopposed. The planes circled London in full view of the crowds in the streets and dropped some 100 bombs near Liverpool Street Station, killing 162 people. It was the worst single attack of the war.

The Zeppelin-Staaken R.VI was one of the heaviest bombers of the war. It could carry a load of 1000 kg. After mid-1917 it flew on raids against London and Paris.

Between the Wars

Within a few years of the first crossing of the English Channel, a host of epic flights had achieved extraordinary feats of endurance and distance. Records seemed to be broken monthly. But the big test, crossing the Atlantic, still beckoned.

In June 1919, John Alcock and Arthur Brown took off from Newfoundland in a modified bomber, the Vickers Vimy. The Vimy had come into service with the British air force just two years before. In Alcock and Brown's version there were two 12-cylinder Rolls-Royce engines giving a top speed of 165 km/h, and a range of 3900 km. It took them 16½ hours to fly non-stop to Ireland where they made a rough landing in a peat bog.

In June 1919, Alcock and Brown crossed the Atlantic in this Vickers Vimy and crash-landed in Ireland.

Round the World

Crossing the Atlantic was an amazing feat, yet barely five years later a team of planes set out to circle the globe. In April 1924, four Douglas World Cruisers (one is shown below) set out from Seattle on the west coast of the United States.

In each plane was a pilot and a mechanic. The planes were fitted with both wheels and floats so they could land anywhere. During the voyage, two of the craft were forced to retire, but the remaining two slogged on to finish the marathon journey. It took them 363 hours to fly the 42,152-km route, at an average speed of 116 km/h. Today it can be done within 48 hours.

Right: In 1924 two Douglas World Cruisers flew around the world. The whole journey took nearly six months.

The Pioneers

The most famous pioneer of them all was Charles Lindbergh. In the early 1920s he had supported his love of flying by working as a stuntman and mail pilot.

When he first suggested flying the Atlantic solo, people were horrified. Planes were still so unreliable at that time that a co-pilot was an essential companion. Besides, flying speeds were so slow it would take over a day to make the crossing.

But Lindbergh was persuasive. He convinced a group of businessmen to back him and build a special plane, the *Spirit of St Louis*.

Charles Lindbergh (above) was born in 1902. He learned to fly as an airmail pilot, flying from St Louis to Chicago. He received a hero's welcome when he landed in Paris. The picture below shows him waving a flag at cheering crowds from the window of the French Aero Club. His solo flight made people appreciate the value of the aeroplane.

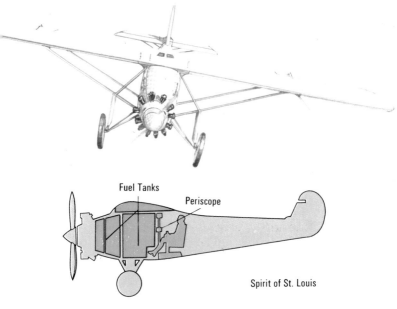

Fuel Tanks

Periscope

Spirit of St. Louis

The *Spirit of St Louis* was a flying fuel tank. In order to save weight, Lindbergh did not take a radio, parachute or sextant. The large fuel tanks took up so much space, Lindbergh had to use a periscope to see ahead.

Crossing the Atlantic

Lindbergh set off from New York on May 20, 1927 with his destination Paris. Flying at an average speed of 172 km/h, he continued through heavy fog and storms and, towards the end of the journey, had to fight to keep himself awake. Since extra fuel tanks had been fitted into the front of the plane, the only way he could look out was through a periscope.

Over the Irish coast he became so excited that he lost his sense of direction and began heading back to America. Correcting his course he continued across southern Britain, the Channel and northern France where crowds watched him fly past. Finally, after a non-stop voyage of 33 hours and 39 minutes he landed in Paris. There, a delirious crowd of 100,000 spectators surrounded his small plane and gave him a triumphant welcome. This was, as the American ambassador in Paris remarked, 'one of history's supreme moments'.

THREE FAMOUS FLIGHTS

During the 1920s, pioneering flights were made to every corner of the globe. In May 1926, two US Navy men flew a three-engined Fokker (1) over the North Pole. In 1928, two Australians and their crew crossed the Pacific in a monoplane named *Southern Cross* (2). Amy Johnson became the first woman to fly solo half way around the world in 1930 when she flew her tiny biplane *Jason* (3) from Britain to Australia.

1

2

3

Today, when most of us take it for granted that we can travel anywhere in the world in a matter of hours, it is hard to recall the difficulties the pioneers faced. Few of them had anything more than a compass by which to steer, and crude maps to guide them. There were no airports and, above all, there were no radios. Once in the air they were entirely alone.

Amelia Earhart was the first woman to fly the Atlantic. She made a solo crossing in 1930. She made many other long-haul solo flights before vanishing without trace over the South Pacific in 1937.

The First Scheduled Flights

The air pioneers hastened the rapid development of aircraft technology between the wars, but, above all, they showed what could be done. Following close behind them were the regular mail and passenger services.

During the 1930s, scheduled flights became common in Europe and North America, while a network of great trunk routes, linking Africa and Asia to Europe, were also established.

The first solo flight around the world was made by Wiley Post in 1933. His Lockheed Vega covered the 24,954-km route in 115 hours, 36 minutes of flying time, but it took him nearly a week and a day, and ten hops, to complete the journey.

Early Airliners

The first commercial airlines after World War I operated mostly with spare war planes. These were converted to contain simple cabins and seats, but for the most part were a rough and uncomfortable way to travel.

Later on, purpose-built airliners came into service. These had heated cabins, seats that were cushioned and a reduced level of noise, made possible by mounting the engines in the wings away from the fuselage.

Since flying speeds were between 160 and 320 km/h, strong headwinds could easily double the time of a journey, and so meals and snacks came to be served by stewards. In a few cases there were even attempts to provide sleeper services, although this never became popular.

Right: The Vickers Vimy, one of the first post-war airliners, was a converted bomber.

Left: In 1919, the French Farman Goliath flew on the first air service between two countries – France and Belgium.

Right: The French Blériot-Spad 33 of the 1920s was slow, small and uncomfortable.

Right: The Fokker FV 11b 3m was a pioneer of monoplane design.

Above: The three-engined Ford Tri-Motor, known affectionately as the 'Tin Goose' first flew in 1926.

Below: The giant HP 42 *Hannibal*, the last of the biplane airliners.

Left: The DC-2 carried 14 passengers and, for the 1930s, was a very advanced plane.

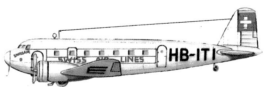

Right: The DH 86, a 1930s biplane, could load up to 16 passengers.

The HP 42 went into service in 1931. This purpose-built airliner had a wingspan of nearly 40 metres. It was used on the long-haul routes from Britain to Egypt, central Africa and to India. It was slow but very safe and comfortable.

The Comfortable Giant

The Handley Page HP 42 was one of the biggest biplanes ever built. It saw service with Imperial Airways, for which eight were made, between 1931 and 1941. These four-engined giants were famous for their safety and reliability. They had two engines mounted on the top wing and two on the bottom. They carried between 24 and 38 passengers depending on the layout of the toilet and galley areas.

The HP 42 set a standard of comfort that was unique for the time. Inside each plane were two well-furnished cabins with cushioned seats and a fixed table separating each facing pair.

Between the cabins were toilets and a galley from which the stewards served three-course meals.

The problems of keeping passengers comfortable on long trunk routes were considerable, as journeys of a week or ten days were not uncommon. The planes could only fly low, had a limited range, and could not travel through the night. In the early 1930s, a maximum of 1120 to 1600 km a day was the best that could be expected, including refuelling stops every 320 to 480 km. Airlines had to build night stopover facilities along the way, often in remote and inhospitable country.

Peacetime Fighters

Below: The Fiat CR 32, a single-seater fighter.

World War I gave aircraft design a terrific boost. In the space of four years planes evolved from being frail, under-powered machines into powerful fighters able to cruise at over 160 km/h, and into giant four-engined bombers that could carry loads of over 1800 kg.

Warplanes Between Wars

After the war, the pace of development slowed down. Fighters that had entered the service in the last months of 1918 were deployed to all parts of the far-flung European empires. Their main task was to patrol borders and help quell local uprisings and, above all, uphold the prestige and authority of the mother country.

The de Havilland DH9A, for example stayed in service with the RAF until the early 1930s. It was a 'general purpose' plane whose roles included bombing and ground attack, ferrying supplies and keeping open lines of communication.

The future development of warplanes, however, could be seen in the aircraft that

Right: The Supermarine S6 raised the world air speed record to over 650 km/h in 1931.

40

Below: The Bristol Bulldog, a mainstay of British military aircraft in the 1920s.

Above left: The Gloster Gladiator, the last of the British biplane fighters.

Above: The Henschel 123 was used as a dive-bomber.

41

battled against each other for the world speed record.

Streamlining for Speed

During the 1920s and 1930s, as racing aircraft were fitted with more powerful engines in the search for extra speed, greater attention began to be paid to streamlining. One of the first changes was to abandon biplane designs for single wing ones. In order to strengthen the body, stressed metal sheeting took the place of wood and fabric.

One of the best examples of this change was the Supermarine S6B. This seaplane won the Schneider Trophy in 1931 with a speed of 651 km/h. The same design team who produced the Supermarine later went on to build the famous Spitfire fighter of World War II.

Firepower

The change from 'stringbag' biplanes with open cockpits to sleek metal monoplanes proceeded slowly. Similarly, there was no rapid change in armament; there were simply too many surplus guns left over from the war.

The big change occurred late in the 1930s when guns began to be grouped in the wings, giving a much greater concentration of firepower.

Below: The Polikarpov I-16, the first low-wing fighter.

Above: The Hawker Fury, first to fly 200 mph in level flight.

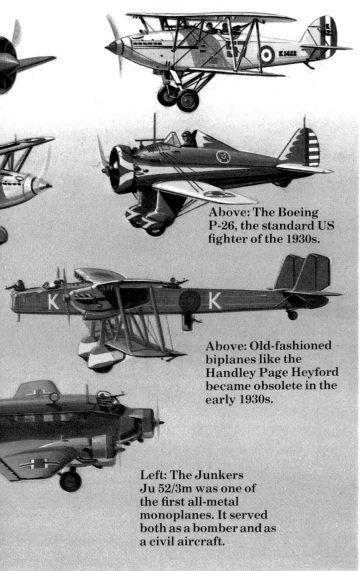

Below: The two-seater single-engined Hawker Hart.

Above: The Boeing P-26, the standard US fighter of the 1930s.

Above: Old-fashioned biplanes like the Handley Page Heyford became obsolete in the early 1930s.

Left: The Junkers Ju 52/3m was one of the first all-metal monoplanes. It served both as a bomber and as a civil aircraft.

World War II

When World War II broke out in 1939, there was no longer any doubt about the vital role of warplanes. Most were now monoplanes. A few flew as fast as 500 km/h, and carried up to eight machine-guns. In the face of such lethal weapons it was obvious that control of the skies was essential.

The Battle of Britain

The Battle of Britain, which began on July 10, 1940, was the first battle ever to be decided entirely by aeroplanes. It was fought over the south of England as bombers and fighters of

Below: The Spitfire was one of the most famous planes in the history of aviation, and perhaps the deadliest fighter of its time. The Spitfire (Mark 1) was in service with 19 RAF squadrons during the Battle of Britain. More than 20,000 were built in over 30 different versions.

the German Luftwaffe battered at their targets in preparation for an invasion by ground forces. Their planes were met by the fighters of the Royal Air Force.

During the first ten days, 657 German aircraft were lost and 153 RAF fighters were shot down. By September, mounting losses convinced Germany to call off the attack. The RAF had won, but only just.

Hawker Hurricane

Messerschmitt Me 109

Top: The Hawker Hurricane first flew in 1935, and at the beginning of the war the RAF had about 300 in service. The sturdy eight-gun Hurricane bore the brunt of the fighting in the Battle of Britain.

Above: The Messerschmitt Bf 109 first entered service with the Luftwaffe in 1937. Armed with machine-guns and cannon, this outstanding plane had a top speed of 689 km/h.

World War II Fighters

At the outbreak of the war, Germany had a large fleet of the world's best fighter plane – the Messerschmitt Me 109. It could outfly the British Hurricane and was only equalled by the Spitfire, which was just starting to go into production. But in the Battle of Britain, RAF pilots had the advantage of flying near their bases. The Me 109s could only carry enough fuel to stay over Britain for 20 to 30 minutes before turning back to base, whereas the Hurricanes and Spitfires could lie in wait for their incoming foe.

The American Mustang
The P-51 Mustang was the most famous fighter used by the United States during World War II. It had a top speed of over 700 km/h and saw action as a long-range fighter escorting bombers on raids against Germany.

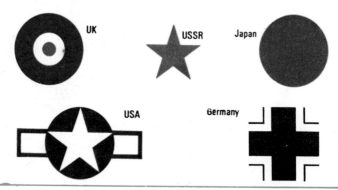

AIRCRAFT INSIGNIA

In 1914, soldiers in the trenches of the Western Front took pot-shots at anything airborne, whether friend or foe. So warplanes began to be marked with their national flags. But, as these could often be confused at a distance, simplified symbols were soon adopted instead.

UK

USSR

Japan

USA

Germany

The Focke-Wulf Fw 190 had a maximum speed of 656 km/h.

The Mustang P-51 was probably the most famous US fighter of World War II.

The American Republic P-47 Thunderbolt had a top speed of 690 km/h.

The Italian Reggiane Re 2000 Falco.

The Russian Mikoyan MiG-3 had a maximum speed of 650 km/h.

The Japanese Nakajima Ki-84 had a maximum speed of 612 km/h.

World War II Bombers

Prior to the war, many people thought that bombers were the most devastating weapons ever invented. Any country would be helpless in the face of massive raids, they claimed, and soon would be forced to surrender to stop the terrible destruction.

As it turned out, in the early months of World War II it was discovered that bombing ground targets was a very hit-and-miss affair. Navigation was very poor, bomb-loads were low and aiming the bombs was extremely inaccurate. It was for this reason that the Germans decided not to make heavy bombers, but to rely on a range of faster medium bombers that were more difficult for fighters to shoot down.

However, as the war became more advanced, the Allies switched to bigger machines. The RAF produced four-engined Stirlings, Halifaxes and Lancasters. The latter were able to carry three times the load of the ageing Wellingtons used early in the war and had a range of 4000 km.

Above:The Russian Ilyushin Il-4 carried a maximum load of 2000 kg. Its maximum range was 4000 km.

Below: The Vickers Wellington bomber was in service with the RAF in 1939, but this twin-engined aircraft was not armed well enough.

Above: The German Dornier Do 217M could carry a bomb-load of 3000 kg over a distance of 2414 km.

The Italian Piaggio P-108B could carry a load of 3500 kg and had a range of 2500 km.

Left: The Avro Lancaster was the backbone of the RAF bombing effort. These aircraft took part in many famous raids. They could carry a maximum load of 6350 kg over a maximum distance of 2670 km.

After the United States came into the war in 1941, her fleets of Mitchells, Liberators and Flying Fortresses were able to deliver an incredible tonnage of bombs onto German targets. Between 1942 and 1945, over 600,000 tonnes of high explosives were rained on German cities and military targets. These raids had considerable effect in hampering Germany's war production.

Above: The North American B-25 Mitchell had a maximum range of 2050 km.

Below: The American B-24 Liberator bomber: load 2268 kg, range 3380 km.

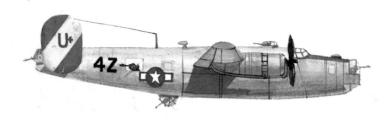

Below: The American Boeing B-29 Superfortress. These heavily armed giant planes had a maximum range of 5230 km and were probably the most effective bombers of the war.

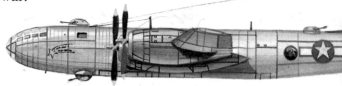

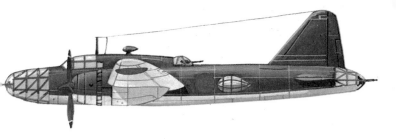

Above: The Mitsubishi Ki-67 Hiryu (Peggy) was a Japanese heavy bomber with a range of 2000 km. It carried a crew of six to eight.

Below: The German Arado Ar 234B jet bomber.

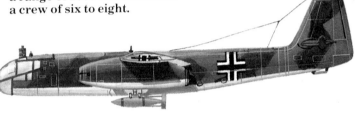

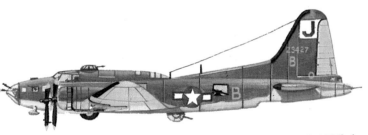

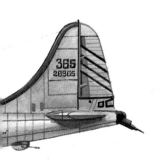

Above: The USAF B-17 Flying Fortress was designed for daylight missions. It carried up to 13 heavy .5-inch machine-guns and had a crew of ten.

Below: The Bell P-59A Airacomet was the first jet aircraft to be produced in the US.

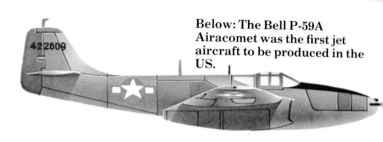

Below: The Gloster Meteor was the first jet to enter service with the RAF. It was the only Allied jet to see service in World War II.

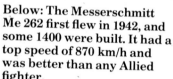

Below: The Messerschmitt Me 262 first flew in 1942, and some 1400 were built. It had a top speed of 870 km/h and was better than any Allied fighter.

Below: The Heinkel 178 made the world's first jet flight in August, 1939. The Heinkel 280 (shown here) was the world's first jet fighter. But it did not go into full production.

The Jet Age

The story of modern jet aircraft began in 1928, when a young RAF officer called Frank Whittle wrote a paper at the RAF College at Cranwell. He foresaw aircraft that would fly at heights where the air is much thinner than at sea level, at speeds of 800 km/h or more. But the Air Ministry was not interested in Whittle's proposals for a jet engine and, by the time he had convinced them of the feasibility of his designs, the Germans had flown the first jet plane – the Heinkel He 178 on August 27, 1939.

Germany then went on to build other and better jets, including the very successful Messerschmitt Me 262 fighter.

Whittle's Ideas Take to the Air

Meanwhile, Whittle had been improving his designs, and on May 15, 1941, the Gloster Company tested his engine in the Gloster-Whittle E28/39. Based on Whittle's ideas, the twin-jet fighter Meteor went into production.

In the United States, Whittle's designs were used to build the Bell P-59 Airacomet, but this was perfected too late to see service in World War II.

Jet aircraft played only a small part in World War II, but their performance was so superior to that of piston-driven aircraft that the days of the propeller-driven plane were clearly numbered.

The first jets were short-range because their turbine engines used so much fuel. They also lacked the instruments, such as advanced radars and gunsights, to match their speeds. However, by the early 1950s designers had solved these problems. Jet bombers and fighters had come to stay.

The Turboprop

When designers first came to consider using jets to power commercial aircraft, they opted for the turboprop or propeller-turbine engine. This successful engine was tested in the Meteor at the end of 1945. Although it did not match up to the pure jet for speed and high-altitude cruising, it was much better than any piston engine.

Fighter Jets of the Fifties

Jet fighters and bombers did not have a chance to prove themselves until the Korean War of 1950–53. By this time, both the United States and Russia had highly effective jet aircraft, including the two famous fighters illustrated below – the US Air Force's F-86 Sabre and Russia's MiG-15.

The prototype Sabre first flew in 1947, and in the following year it became the first US warplane to break the sound barrier. The single-seat, single-engined F-86 became the USAF's first operational swept-wing fighter.

During the Korean War, the Sabre and the MiG-15 met in the first-ever, all-jet dog-fights. Although the MiG had a slightly better performance, American pilots gained the upper hand. When production of the F-86 ended in 1958, more of these planes had been made than any other Western warplane.

The MiG-15

This stumpy little swept-wing jet fighter became Russia's standard aircraft after the Korean War. Between 15,000 and 18,000 of these successful aircraft were built from 1947 onwards. Although this simple, well-armed fighter is now obsolete, it is still flown by the air forces of many countries.

MiG-15

F-86 Sabre

The French Mirage III first flew in 1956. Today, it carries air-to-air missiles and twin 30-mm cannons.

The Il-28 of 1948 (centre) was Russia's first jet bomber. The MiG-21 of 1955 (bottom) is still much in use.

The three aircraft illustrated here appeared in the late 40s and early 50s. The French Mirage, fast, agile, well-armed and cheap, became one of the most successful of all jet fighters.

Russia's Il-28 was produced in 1948. In 1959, the MiG-21 became the world's fastest plane, with a speed of 2388 km/h. Today, it carries up to four air-to-air missiles, a twin-barrelled 23-mm cannon and attachment points for bombs or for rocket pods.

The Airliners

Until the 1930s, most air-liners were simply converted bombers or large biplanes with open flight decks and a few seats inside. Then, in 1933, the first all-metal air-liner entered service in the United States – the Boeing 247.

The Boeing 247 would be better remembered had it not been followed by several

Vickers Viscount, the best medium-range air-liner of the 50s and 60s.

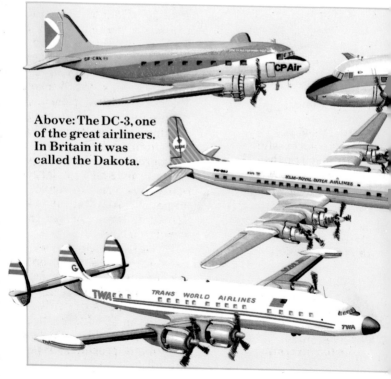

Above: The DC-3, one of the great airliners. In Britain it was called the Dakota.

The Fokker Friendship, one of the best-selling turboprop airliners.

Above: Vickers Viking, a successful plane based on the Wellington bomber.

Left: The DC-7, Douglas's answer to the Constellation.

Left: Lockheed Super Constellation, one of the last and best of the long-range propeller aircraft.

famous Douglas aircraft, especially the Douglas DC-3. This great plane was produced in large numbers, many of them still in service.

But it was the Vickers Viscount which was the most successful medium-range airliner of the time. This four-engined aircraft was a turboprop – a type of jet engine in which a larger turbine is used to drive a propeller. A total of 444 Viscounts were sold to the world's airlines.

Turbocharged engines were used for 100-seater giants like the Boeing Stratocruiser, the Lockheed Super Constellation and the Douglas DC-7. Cruising at 700 km/h, these aircraft were among the last in a line of propeller-driven aircraft.

Jet Airliners

The first jet airliner flew on July 27, 1949. It was the de Havilland Comet. This spectacularly successful plane entered service with BOAC in May 1952, and would have continued to make history had it not been for a series of accidents in 1954. These accidents were traced to metal fatigue and all Comets were grounded.

Before the fault could be put right de Havilland had lost its lead. America's Boeing 707s and Douglas DC-8s were about to appear.

The Two-engined Jets
On these pages are illustrated some two-engined jets

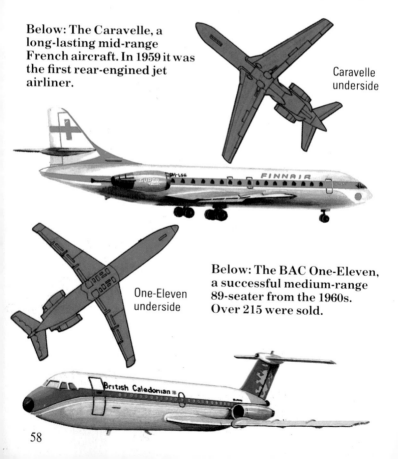

Below: The Caravelle, a long-lasting mid-range French aircraft. In 1959 it was the first rear-engined jet airliner.

Caravelle underside

One-Eleven underside

Below: The BAC One-Eleven, a successful medium-range 89-seater from the 1960s. Over 215 were sold.

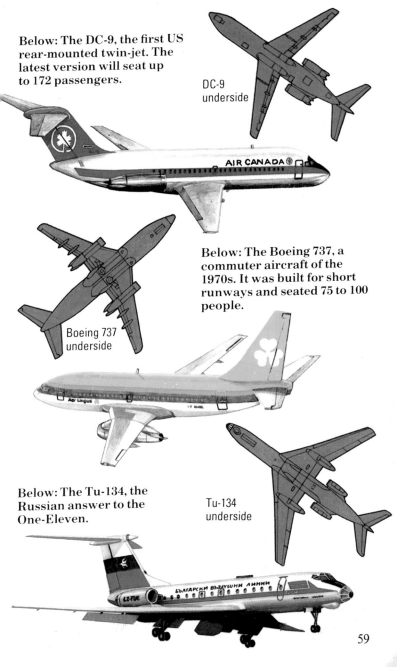

Below: The DC-9, the first US rear-mounted twin-jet. The latest version will seat up to 172 passengers.

DC-9 underside

AIR CANADA

Below: The Boeing 737, a commuter aircraft of the 1970s. It was built for short runways and seated 75 to 100 people.

Boeing 737 underside

Aer Lingus

Below: The Tu-134, the Russian answer to the One-Eleven.

Tu-134 underside

БЪЛГАРСКИ ВЪЗДУШНИ ЛИНИИ

59

designed for short- and medium-distance routes. They are usually smaller than the three- and four-engined jets, though not necessarily slower.

The Big Jets

The huge increase in the number of passengers in the 1960s meant that airliners had to increase in size. Two three-engined aircraft made their appearance – the Boeing 727 and the Hawker Siddeley Trident, which took the place of the Comet in 1964. Russia's Tu-154 – the 'Tupolev Trident' – followed in 1971.

Above: The Boeing 727 tri-jet uses many of the same parts as the 707, and has been stretched to give a 3000-km range.

Above: The Hawker Siddeley Trident has a range of 1600 km at a speed of 1000 km/h. This tri-jet can seat between 100 and 150 people.

Below: A300B, the European airbus, has seats for 345 people on short- and medium-haul routes.

Airbus A300B underside

156

AIR FRANCE

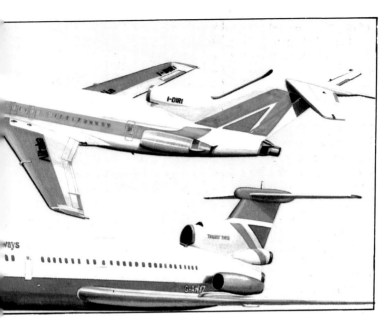

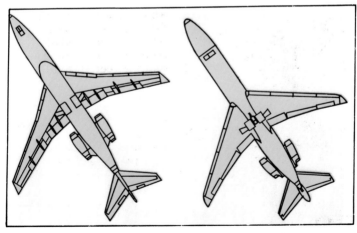

Undersides of Boeing 727 (left) and Trident (right).

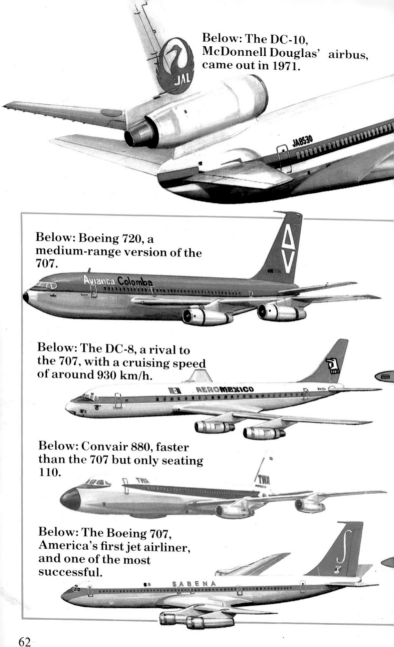

Below: The DC-10, McDonnell Douglas' airbus, came out in 1971.

Below: Boeing 720, a medium-range version of the 707.

Below: The DC-8, a rival to the 707, with a cruising speed of around 930 km/h.

Below: Convair 880, faster than the 707 but only seating 110.

Below: The Boeing 707, America's first jet airliner, and one of the most successful.

Undersides of planes:
above, DC-10; left from top,
Boeing 720, DC-8, Convair 880,
Boeing 707.

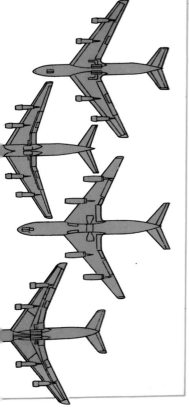

Meanwhile, powerful new turbofan engines have produced the 400-seat TriStar and DC-10, both wide-bodied 'airbuses' which have been stretched for use on long-distance flights.

The Four-engined Jets

The first successful four-engined jets were the Boeing 707 and the Douglas DC-8. When the 707 entered service in 1958, people thought it would fail. No airline could fill its 130 seats. Yet, by the 1960s the 707 had been stretched to carry 189 passengers. And the DC-8 was soon being built to seat 250 people.

63

Giants of the Air

The first 'jumbo jet' was the Boeing 747, which went into service with Pan American in 1970. This huge aircraft weighed twice as much as any previous airliner. Each of its four engines produced 19,700 kg of thrust, it had a range of 10,424 km and a cruising speed of 978 km/h.

The 747 can carry up to 490 passengers. Its huge cabin is 6 metres wide and 56 metres long, with a headroom of over 2½ metres. Although it can take almost 500 passengers, the basic model seats only 374 people in comfort.

The Airbuses

After the Boeing 747 came the airbuses – the McDonnell Douglas DC-10 and the Lockheed L-1011 TriStar. These wide-bodied jets work economically over short and medium distances. Both have three engines, with one turbofan mounted beneath each wing and the third at the tail. They can carry more than 300 passengers.

The A-300B is a European airbus, slightly smaller than the DC-10 and L-1011. It has two turbofan engines.

Above: The Boeing 747
'jumbo jet' from 1970. At a
maximum weight of 356
tonnes, the 747 is the world's
biggest airliner.

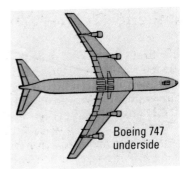

Boeing 747
underside

Below: Lockheed's L-1011
TriStar is similar to the
DC-10. It has a cruising speed
of over 900 km/h. It has also
been stretched to a long-haul
400-seater.

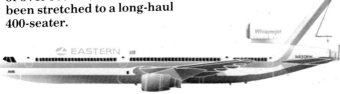

Faster Than Sound

Aircraft that travel faster than the speed of sound are called 'supersonic'. To reach this speed they must pass through the shock waves of the so-called 'sound barrier'. Above a height of about 11,000 metres the air is 'thin' and the sound barrier is around 1060 km/h. Supersonic aircraft can travel in comfort at this height provided they are designed to withstand the shock waves.

Concorde and Tu-144

Both the world's supersonic airliners – Concorde and the Russian Tu-144 – are masterpieces of aerodynamic design. They both have swept wings, as this dart shape is best for high-speed control. They can cruise at over 2000 km/h for almost three hours, and both seat 140 passengers.

Military aircraft now fly at speeds of three and four times the speed of sound. As long ago as 1967 the American X-15 rocket plane reached a speed of over 7200 km/h.

Concorde can cruise at Mach 2.04 – over twice the speed of sound – at high altitude.

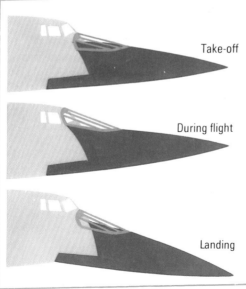

Take-off

During flight

Landing

At take-off and in flight Concorde's nose is kept straight. But because of the wing-shape, the plane lands at a very sharp angle. The front is pointed so high that, unless the nose were dropped, the pilot would be unable to see the runway.

Modern Military Aircraft

Air power is now of supreme military importance. Supersonic combined fighter and bomber planes are so well equipped with computers that they can practically fly themselves. Planes like the American SR-71 Blackbird zoom around the Earth at three times the speed of sound at a height of 19 km. Their spy cameras can focus on an object the size of a golf ball anywhere on the Earth's surface. The Blackbird's cameras, radars and infra-red sensors can map 155,000 sq km of the Earth's surface in an hour.

Right: The USAF's SR-71 Blackbird is one of the world's most sophisticated warplanes. It has flown at over 3330 km/h and reached a sustained height of over 24 km.

Below: Russia's big advanced interceptor, the MiG-25, travels at three times the speed of sound.

Above: The Anglo-French Jaguar strike bomber and reconnaissance fighter.

Right: America's latest advanced lightweight fighter, the F-16.

Above: The F-104 Starfighter supersonic fighter and fighter-bomber.

Below: Britain's Buccaneer, one of the world's best low-level strike bombers.

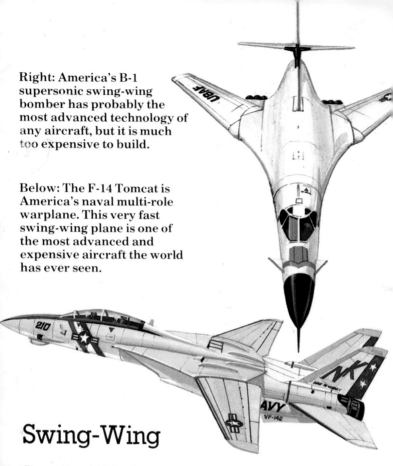

Right: America's B-1 supersonic swing-wing bomber has probably the most advanced technology of any aircraft, but it is much too expensive to build.

Below: The F-14 Tomcat is America's naval multi-role warplane. This very fast swing-wing plane is one of the most advanced and expensive aircraft the world has ever seen.

Swing-Wing

Since the 1960s there have been many improvements in aircraft design – at fantastic cost. Perhaps the outstanding new feature of some fighting planes has been the swing-wing.

Swept-back, or delta, wings are ideal for supersonic flight, as they minimize the 'drag' of the air. But straight-out wings, although they have high drag, provide a lot of lift for easier slow-speed manoeuvring, landing and take-off. So, to ensure that supersonic aircraft have the best wing-plan at all times, the logical solution was to design planes with wings that can be moved as required between straight and delta positions while in flight.

Left: Backfire, Russia's equivalent to the B-1.

Left: The European Tornado Multi-Role Combat Aircraft (MRCA) is designed to do the jobs of several types of warplanes.

Right: America's F-111 strike fighter was the world's first swing-wing warplane.

A cutaway of the F-14 Tomcat swing-wing fighter. It is powered by two Pratt and Whitney turbofans, and has retractable fins fitted to each side of the engine housings to keep the aircraft stable in flight while the wings are changing their position. The prototype F-14 flew in December 1970. By 1974 the first full squadron was flying from the carrier USS *Enterprise*. Each of these aircraft cost around $20 million.

Slats

Retracting Undercarriage

VHF Antenna

Martin-Baker Ejection Seats

Armored Glass Screen

Upward Folding Radome

Radar Scanner

Retractable Air-Refuelling Probe

Fuel Tanks

Ammunition Tank (1000 Rounds)

Retractable Glove Va

Folding Boarding Ladder

Retracting Nose Wheels

Collision Beacon

Infra-Red Seeker

Six-Barrel Rotary Gun

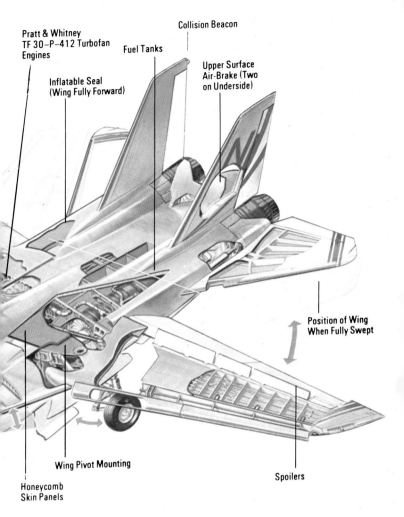

Pratt & Whitney
TF 30-P-412 Turbofan
Engines

Fuel Tanks

Collision Beacon

Upper Surface
Air-Brake (Two
on Underside)

Inflatable Seal
(Wing Fully Forward)

Position of Wing
When Fully Swept

Wing Pivot Mounting

Spoilers

Honeycomb
Skin Panels

The first swing-wing warplane was the USAF's F-111 fighter of 1964. This technical advance has since become popular in both Russia and the US, as well as being used in aircraft such as the European Tornado MRCA.

The latest designs feature automatic computer-control of the wing setting to suit the conditions of flight.

73

Helicopters Today

Helicoptors get both lift and thrust from their spinning wings, called rotors. The first efficient helicoptors appeared in the 1950s, and since then their uses have increased steadily.

As they are the only aircraft that can hover at any height and move up and down vertically, they have been used to rescue people from sinking ships, burning buildings and other potential disasters. They are also used to take bulky loads to inaccessible places. Some airlines operate helicoptor services between airports and city centres.

In addition, 'choppers' have many military uses. They are used as gunships, assault troop transports, submarine hunters, and rescue aircraft.

Below: The British Royal Navy's Sea King – a multi-purpose assault, transport and rescue helicopter – cruises at 193 km/h.

Below: The Anglo-French Westland Lynx is one of the world's most advanced submarine hunter-killers. Cruise speed 283 km/h.

Below: The Huey Cobra earned itself a reputation for speed, surprise and killing power as a gunship in Vietnam.

Below: Russia's latest gunship, the Mil-24, carries a formidable array of weapons.

75

Further Facts

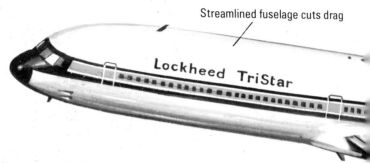

Streamlined fuselage cuts drag

Lockheed TriStar

How a Plane Flies

This Lockheed TriStar is a typical modern jetliner. Yet exactly the same principles of flight apply to it as to the Wright brothers' *Flyer* in 1903.

In flight, there are four main forces acting on any aeroplane. *Lift* is created by air flowing over the wings. *Thrust* is provided by the engines as they push it forward through the air. Both these forces help a plane to stay aloft. *Drag* is the resistance of the air as the plane flies through it, while *weight* is the pull of Earth's gravity. These last two forces slow a plane and pull it back down.

In order to fly, a plane's engines have to push it forward fast enough to overcome drag, and its wings have to generate enough lift to overcome the pull of

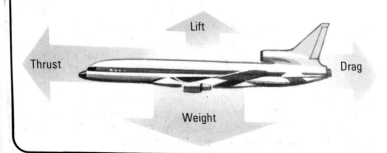

Lift

Thrust

Drag

Weight

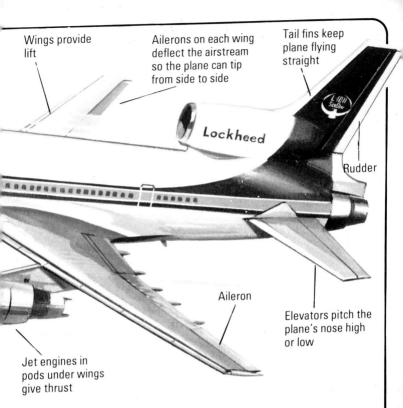

Wings provide lift

Ailerons on each wing deflect the airstream so the plane can tip from side to side

Tail fins keep plane flying straight

Lockheed

L-1011 TriStar

Rudder

Aileron

Elevators pitch the plane's nose high or low

Jet engines in pods under wings give thrust

gravity. If either drag or weight is greater than thrust and lift, then the plane slows and drops out of the sky.

The Lifting Power of a Wing
The shape of a typical aircraft wing reveals the secret of its lifting power. The upper surface is more curved than the lower surface; in other words it is longer. Air flowing over the upper surface has to accelerate to catch up with the air flowing underneath. This 'stretches' the air on top, making it thinner and reducing its pressure. This low pressure area on the top of the wing contrasts with the high pressure on the bottom. The high pressure pushes the wing up – known as *lift*.

Different kinds of wings have different purposes. Fast planes usually have much thinner wings than slow-flying ones.

The Cockpit

The picture on the right shows the cockpit of a modern airliner; in this case a Boeing 747. The captain sits in the left-hand seat, the co-pilot on the right. The flight engineer, who looks after the engine and other systems, sits in the third seat before a bank of instruments.

Although the cockpit looks impossibly cluttered with dials and switches, the basic flying controls and instruments are the same as in all other aircraft.

The Flying Controls

The two most important flying controls are the column and the rudder. The column, or 'stick', in a 747 looks much like the steering wheel of a car. It controls the pitch and roll of the plane.

Pushed forwards, it tilts the elevators down and pitches the plane nose-down into a dive. Pulled back, it tilts the elevators up, pitching the plane into a climb.

By moving the control column from side to side, the ailerons move up and down. If the column is pushed left, the aileron on that side moves up while that on the right goes down. The plane then rolls left.

The rudder pedals are operated by the pilot's feet. Pushing the right one moves the rudder and turns the plane's nose to the right. The left one does the opposite.

Using these basic controls, together with the engines' thrust, the pilot can climb, dive, turn and bank.

THE INSTRUMENTS

The altimeter measures air pressure just like a barometer. It translates this into a reading of the plane's height.

The airspeed indicator measures the plane's speed through the air in knots (one knot is 1.85 km/h), via a hollow probe called a pilot tube which sticks out into the airstream.

The artificial horizon tells the pilot whether he is flying straight and level or is banking and sinking.

ALTIMETER

Here the plane is cruising at 10,650 ft (3246 metres)

AIRSPEED INDICATOR

ARTIFICIAL HORIZON

The plane is travelling at
290 knots (536 km/h)

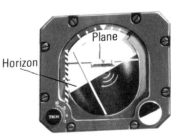

Instrument shows the plane
is banking to the right

Emergency!

Flying is a remarkably safe way to travel. The world 'fatal crash' rate is just over two per million flights. A fatal crash is one in which one or more people are killed.

But accidents do happen — over 1,500 passengers and crew died in the USA alone between 1973 and 1978. So all airliners are equipped with various items of emergency gear like the ones shown on these pages.

Life Rafts

Planes that fly over water carry self-inflating rubber life rafts. The one shown at the top of the page can take 26 people. The raft carries food, paddles, a radio, flares and bright red marker dyes with which to signal rescuers.

Escape Chutes

The Lockheed TriStar (right) has emergency exit chutes, like other airliners, for making quick escapes. The chutes extend themselves automatically once the crew release them. When tested by Lockheed, a full plane of 380 people could be emptied in 90 seconds using all the chutes (four to each side). Escape must be this swift, as in fires more people die from poisonous fumes from the

A Lockheed TriStar with its four starboard escape chutes fully extended

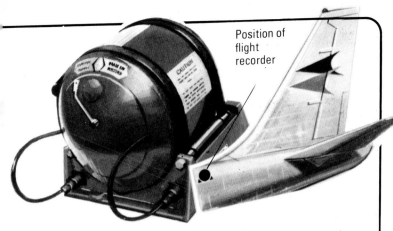

Position of flight recorder

plastic cabin furnishings than from the flames.

Flight Recorders

Flight recorders (above) were first put into planes in the 1960s. They continually record vital details of the flight, such as speed and height. A tape of the crew's conversations is made as well. If a crash occurs, the flight recorder can give vital clues as to the way it happened.

At any one time the recorder only has the previous 30 minutes of the flight on tape. Anything before that is wiped out automatically and the tape used again. Flight recorders are very tough. The one above can withstand an impact of two tonnes and can survive a fire of 1,000°C for half an hour. They are also called 'black boxes'.

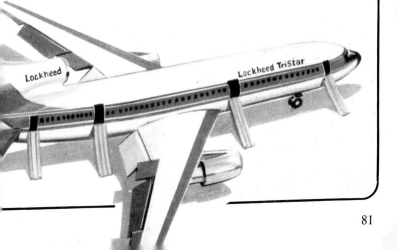

Lockheed

Lockheed TriStar

The New Airships

The three airships on this page are modern descendants of the giants of the 1920s and 1930s. Ever since the crash of the R101 near Beauvais in France, on October 6, 1930, airship development has remained at a standstill. But modern materials and the search to save fuel has, perhaps, given the airship a chance to come back.

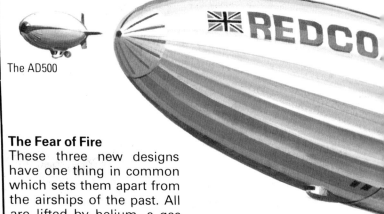

The AD500

The Fear of Fire

These three new designs have one thing in common which sets them apart from the airships of the past. All are lifted by helium, a gas which is non-flammable. Previous airships all used hydrogen. This is lighter than helium, and so has a greater lifting power, but it catches fire extremely easily.

The disastrous consequences of using hydrogen were tragically shown by the crash of the *Hindenburg* in 1937. The whole ship was consumed in a ball of flame in a matter of minutes. Even with safety measures like special steel-lined smoking compartments, the dangers of using hydrogen are never resolved. For this reason, modern airship designs all shun hydrogen.

Airship Jumbos

The little AD500, above left, was produced by two British designers. Sadly, the ship was damaged in a sudden storm. But its engineers have now joined forces with Airship Industries, a company

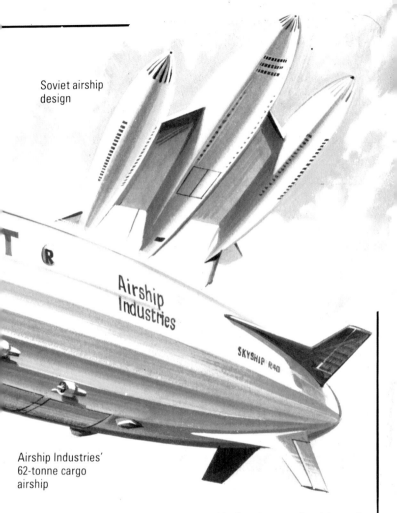

Soviet airship design

Airship Industries' 62-tonne cargo airship

that expects airships to have a great future. The most spectacular model it plans to build is the 62-tonne cargo ship shown above.

Looming over it in the background is an airship idea from the USSR. This triple-hulled monster is driven by a submarine-type atomic power plant. It is designed to carry 1600 passengers or 300 tonnes of cargo. This monster, if it is ever built, would be able to circle the globe at a steady 380 km/h.

Flying Boats

The golden age of flying boats was in the 1920s and 1930s. This was the era when long-haul routes were being pioneered across the oceans of the world. The notion of a plane with a boat hull was a perfect answer to the lack of airports in remote regions and to the risks of having to make forced landings *en route*. In effect, the sea became one big runway.

A Flying Giant
One of the biggest flying boat designs was the giant Dornier Do-X. This German plane was powered by a phalanx of 12 engines set on top of the huge wing. It could take off with 150 passengers and ten crew aboard and, as happened on its maiden flight, an extra nine stowaways.

The Do-X would cruise exceptionally low, sometimes less than 30 metres, above the waves. The cushion of air which builds up under aircraft at low levels, known as the 'ground effect' helped give extra lift and so extend the plane's range.

The Water Bomber
During World War II, hundreds of military airstrips

Dornier Do-X

D-1929

Canadair CL-215

were built around the world. This, combined with greatly improved cruising ranges and the ability of planes to fly high above the weather, sounded the death-knell for the flying-boat design.

But modern specialist planes are still produced that carry on the tradition, if only in a very limited way. The Canadair CL-215 water bomber, is a twin-engined flying boat able to swoop down onto lakes and rivers and scoop up thousands of litres of water in one swift operation.

It then flies over fires and bombs them with water. This technique is widely used to fight remote forest fires in Canada and also in the south of France.

Twelve engines, mounted in six separate units on top of the wing

DO-X

Bigger Still

The history of aviation can be summed up as the search for bigger and faster aircraft. Although expensive fuels have meant that speeds, today, have reached a plateau, planes continue to grow.

The Biggest of All

More than a decade after its maiden flight, the biggest commercial jet is still the Boeing 747. This giant holds a string of impressive records related to its exceptional size.

In 1974, a record 674 people were crammed aboard a Qantas 747 to be air-lifted out of hurricane-torn Darwin in the north of Australia. Compared to this a more usual load is 320 economy class passengers and 50 first-class. But British Airways have designs for a stretched version able to carry 1000 passengers!

The main deck of a 747 is 57 metres long. This is greater than the distance flown by the Wright brothers

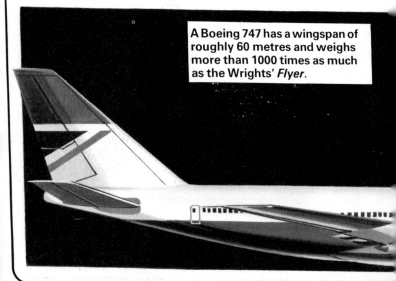

A Boeing 747 has a wingspan of roughly 60 metres and weighs more than 1000 times as much as the Wrights' *Flyer*.

The Wright brothers' *Flyer* covered 37 metres on its first flight, 20 metres less than the length of the 747's main deck.

at Kitty Hawk. There is room on a second upstairs deck for another 16 people. The total passenger and crew area is almost as much as two tennis courts.

On take-off, a fully-loaded 747-200B weighs over 365,000 kg. Nearly half of this load is fuel, an amount sufficient to run a small car for four years. Every hour, the four engines gulp 11,000 kg of fuel. Yet the number of people it carries is so great that it is still one of the more economical ways to travel.

At take-off, a Jumbo is moving at 293 km/h. During climb this rises to 465 km/h and at cruising height peaks at 920 km/h, although headwinds can make a big difference.

The Douglas DC-3 first saw service early in the 1930s. It carried 21 passengers at about 350 km/h.

Vertical Take-Off

Harrier Gr.5

Modern high-speed warplanes need long concrete runways on which to land and take off. The great drawback, of course, is that runways make easy targets. A bombed runway will trap an entire squadron on the ground, leaving the planes vulnerable to attack.

The VTOL

One solution to this problem is to build a fighter that can land and take off vertically. When the Harrier Gr.1 came into service with the RAF in 1969, it was the world's first Vertical Take Off and Landing (VTOL) warplane.

The key to this warplane is a set of four swivelling nozzles. The jet exhaust can be directed through them, either to point backwards or to point downwards depending on whether the pilot wishes to fly forward or to climb straight into the air.

The Harrier Gr.5 (above) is the latest version to leave the drawing board. It has bigger wings than its predecessors, making it more manoeuvrable and giving it the ability to carry more bombs and rockets. At its nose is a laser attachment that guides 'smart' bombs to their targets.

Hitching a Lift

A novel, but amazingly simple concept that has been suggested recently is to launch fighters from small ships by using helicopters to get them airborne.

Many navy vessels nowadays are fitted with a helipad. A slightly larger helipad than the one they use at present would allow them to carry a small fighter, such as the F-18 Hornet (below). A big navy helicopter could lift it off the deck, carry it along until launch speed had been reached and then let it go.

To land, the helicopter would snag the fighter from the air, then lower it by winch back to the deck.

F-18 Hornet

Planes of the Future

With the prospect that we will be living with oil shortages before the end of the century, the greatest problem of the future will be to ensure that planes have plentiful and reliable sources of fuel.

Hydrogen Fuel

One suggestion is to adapt jet engines to burn pure hydrogen. Since this is a bulky gas in normal conditions it would have to be loaded into fuel tanks in super-cold liquid form. The attraction of hydrogen is that it burns very efficiently, is very cheap and can be pro- duced in unlimited amounts from water. There is already a project underway by Lockheed to convert the TriStar into a hydrogen-burning airliner.

A New Strength

A development that may have a great impact on future warplanes is the use of carbon-fibre to build wings. As this material is far stronger than metal, it would permit forward-sweep designs to be used for the first time. This shape gives more lift and manoeuvrability and also makes it possible to build smaller craft without losing any firepower. Such a plane could out-turn a conventional fighter quite easily (see diagram below) and then bring it down with a missile.

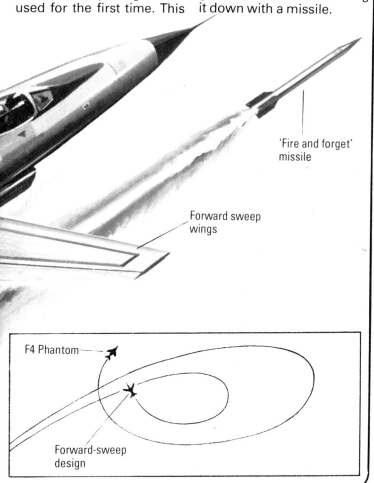

'Fire and forget' missile

Forward sweep wings

F4 Phantom

Forward-sweep design

INDEX

Page numbers in *italics* refer to illustrations

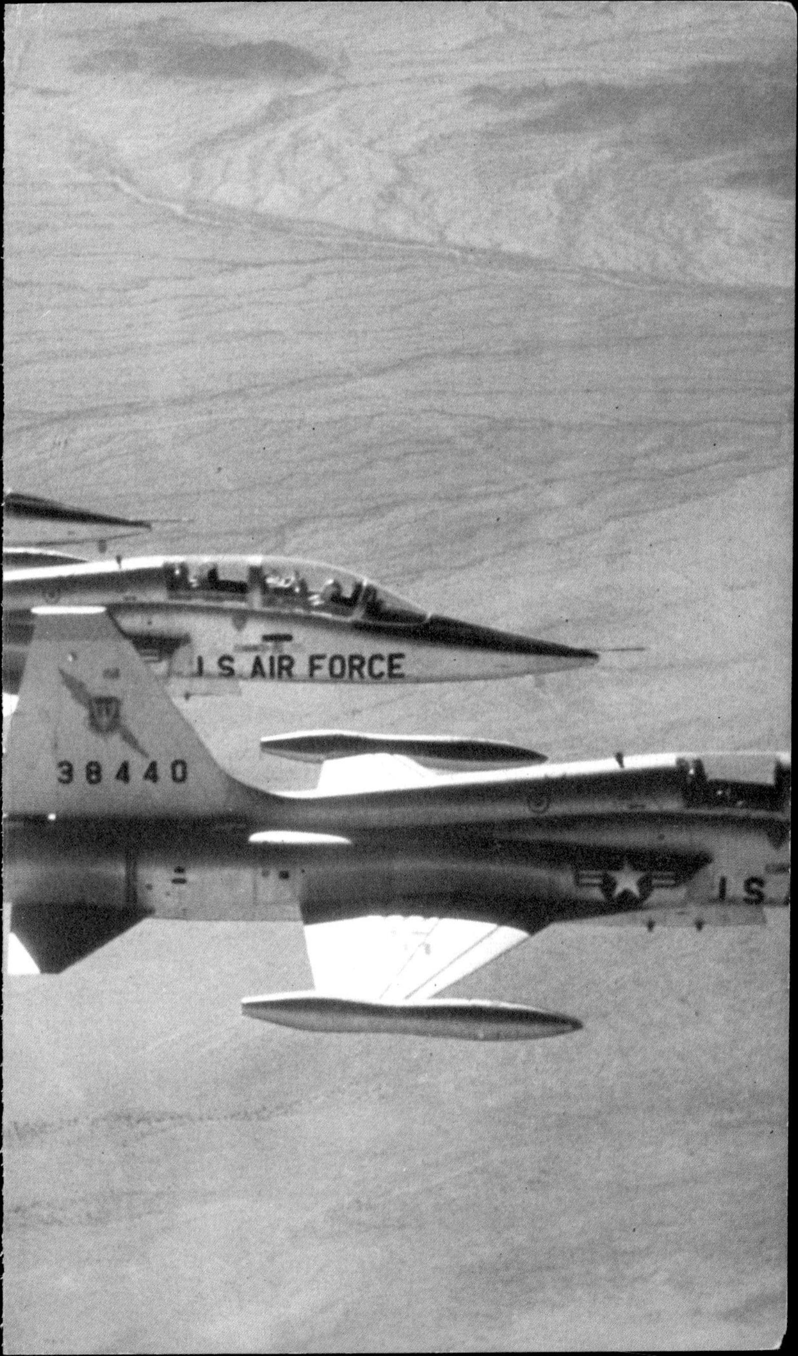

I S AIR FORCE
38440
I S

Piccolo Explorer Books

Titles include:
Animal Homes
Animal Journeys
The Age of Dinosaurs
The Age of Steam
The Planets
Knights and Castles
The World of Speed
The World of Robots
The Great Ice Age
War and Weapons
Under the Sea
The Midnight World
UFOs
The Violent Earth

Wildlife
The Penguin
The Tiger
The Kangaroo
The Beaver
The Bear
The Wolf
The Hedgehog
The Butterfly

History Makers
Napoleon Bonaparte
Joan of Arc
Genghis Khan
Conquerors of Everest

Guides
Birds
Horses and Ponies
Airliners
Arms and Armour
Shells
Dogs
Racing Cars
Wild Flowers
Trees
Spacecraft
Cats
Insects
Combat Aircraft
Fighting Ships
Military Uniforms
Tanks

Mysteries
Fabulous Beasts
Sea Mysteries
Lost Cities
Missing Treasure
Ghosts
Devils and Demons

Secrets
Secrets of Nature
Secrets of the Sea
Secrets of Space
Secrets of the Human Body